NEW

The three Billy Goats Gruff

Illustrated by Val Biro

Nelson

Storyteller

Little Billy Goat Gruff

Middle Billy Goat Gruff

Great Big Billy Goat Gruff

The Troll

Once upon a time there were
three goats who lived
on the side of a hill.
They did not have much to eat.
On the other side of
the bridge was a hill
covered in green grass.

I am Little Billy Goat Gruff.
I am very hungry.

I am Middle Billy Goat Gruff.
I am very hungry.

I am Great Big Billy Goat Gruff.
I am big and strong.

The grass on this hill has
all been eaten.
Why can't we go over
the bridge and eat the grass
on the hill over there?

Under the bridge lives a Troll.
If you try to cross
the bridge he will
eat you for his supper.

He sits under the bridge.
Every day he waits for
someone to cross his bridge.

You must stay with us and
you must not cross the bridge.

I am the Troll who
lives under the bridge.
No one can cross my bridge.
I will eat them for my supper.

So the three Billy Goats Gruff stayed on the hill.
Then one day Little Billy Goat Gruff looked at the green grass on the other hill.

I am going to cross
the bridge.
I am not afraid of the Troll.
I am too small for a supper.

So Little Billy Goat Gruff
went trip trap over the
rickety rackety bridge.

Who's that going trip trap over my rickety rackety bridge?

It's only me,
Little Billy Goat Gruff.
I am going to eat the
green grass on the other hill.

Stop. No one goes over my rickety rackety bridge.
I shall eat you for my supper.

Oh please don't eat me Mr Troll. Wait for Middle Billy Goat Gruff. There is much more supper on him.

Oh very well.
You may go over my bridge.
I shall wait for
Middle Billy Goat Gruff.

So Little Billy Goat Gruff
went on over the rickety
rackety bridge to eat
the green grass on the hill.

Then Middle Billy Goat Gruff
saw Little Billy Goat Gruff
eating the grass on
the other side of the bridge.

Look, Great Big Billy Goat
Gruff.   Little Billy Goat Gruff
is eating the green grass on
the other side of the bridge.

I am not afraid of the Troll.
I shall go over the bridge.

So Middle Billy Goat Gruff went trip trap, trip trap over the rickety rackety bridge.

14

Who's that going trip trap
over my rickety rackety
bridge?

It's only me,
Middle Billy Goat Gruff.
I am going to eat the
green grass on the other hill.

Stop. No one goes over
my rickety rackety bridge.
I shall eat you for my supper.

Oh please don't do that
Mr Troll. Wait for
Great Big Billy Goat Gruff.
There is much more supper
on him.

Oh very well.
You may go over my bridge.
I shall wait for
Great Big Billy Goat Gruff.

So Middle Billy Goat Gruff
went on over the rickety
rackety bridge to eat
the green grass on the hill.

Soon Great Big
Billy Goat Gruff saw
Little Billy Goat Gruff and
Middle Billy Goat Gruff
eating the grass on
the other side of the bridge.

I am not afraid of the Troll.
I shall go over the bridge.

So Great Big Billy Goat Gruff went trip trap, trip trap over the rickety rackety bridge.

Who's that going trip trap over my rickety rackety bridge?

I am Great Big Billy Goat Gruff.
I am going to eat the grass on
the other hill.

Stop.   No one goes over
my rickety rackety bridge.
I am going to eat you
for my supper.

Oh no you are not.
We shall see about that.

Then Great Big Billy Goat
Gruff put down his head and
he ran trip trap at the Troll.
He tossed the Troll up
into the air.

Ow. Ow. Ow.

The Troll fell into the water and was never seen again. Then Great Big Billy Goat Gruff went trip trap over the bridge to eat the green grass on the hill.

I am not hungry now.

I am not hungry now.

And no one will eat us for supper now.

So the three Billy Goats Gruff ate the green grass on the other side of the bridge and they all lived happily ever after.